Praise for Corey Elizabeth Jackson's
Death Kindly Stopped For Me:
A Book of Poetry Inspired by Emily Dickinson

"Though these poems take Dickinson as their starting point, what we find here is a poet fully herself. This is a delightful collection, always intriguing, and full of surprises."

~ Michael Martin, editorial consultant for *Angelico Press*

"There is no dearth of poetry inspired by Dickinson, but I was particularly struck by the poetry of Corey Elizabeth Jackson, who is inspired by Dickinson's poetry of Death and finds an unusual solace and even cheerfulness in it."

~ Ivy Schweitzer, professor emerita of English at *Dartmouth College* and an editor at *The Emily Dickinson International Society Bulletin*

"Readers will find an approach to life and Death that will bring comfort and empathy, along with a word of encouragement, on every page. It is a collection worth reading and comes with my own enthusiastic recommendation."

~ James A. Tweedie, First Place Winner, *The Society of Classical Poets' 2021 International Poetry Competition*

"This book of poetry and its beautiful artwork is a keeper . . . for Emily Dickinson students and teachers, for classical poetry lovers, art lovers and soul seekers alike!"

~ Dayna Dunbar, award-winning novelist, author of *Awake: The Legacy of Akara*

Death Kindly Stopped For Me

Death Kindly Stopped For Me

A Book of Poetry

Inspired by Emily Dickinson

Corey Elizabeth Jackson

PLATYPUS
PUBLISHING

Platypus Publishing
http://www.platypusbooks.com

Names: Jackson, Corey Elizabeth, author.
Title: Death Kindly Stopped for Me: A Book of Poetry Inspired by Emily Dickinson / Corey Elizabeth Jackson.
Description: Austin, Texas: Platypus, 2024
Identifiers:
ISBN 978-1-965016-16-9 (paperback)

Cover design and illustrations by Daniel Schmelling
Interior design by Ashley Santoro
Editing by Michael Martin
Marketing by Liz Dubelman

To the MacHarts ~ Jon, Stefphanie, Riddick and Rowghan

~ In Eternity

Unable are the Loved to die
For Love is Immortality,
Nay, it is Deity —

Unable they that love — to die
For Love reforms Vitality
Into Divinity.

~ Emily Dickinson

I think love is the single
most important word in
the human language.

~ Barbra Streisand

Contents

IV. Soulscape

Because I could not stop for Death

BY EMILY DICKINSON

Because I could not stop for Death –
He kindly stopped for me –
The Carriage held but just Ourselves –
And Immortality.

We slowly drove – He knew no haste
And I had put away
My labor and my leisure too,
For His Civility –

We passed the School, where Children strove
At Recess – in the Ring –
We passed the Fields of Gazing Grain –
We passed the Setting Sun –

Or rather – He passed Us –
The Dews drew quivering and Chill –
For only Gossamer, my Gown –
My Tippet – only Tulle –

We paused before a House that seemed
A Swelling of the Ground –
The Roof was scarcely visible –
The Cornice – in the Ground –

Since then – 'tis Centuries – and yet
Feels shorter than the Day
I first surmised the Horses' Heads
Were toward Eternity –

Introduction

The intricate layers of meaning in Emily Dickinson's poem "Because I could not stop for Death" shimmer and cascade indelibly in my mind. They trickle into grooves that spread ever more deeply into my consciousness. Stopping for Death? Who does that? Doesn't Death just happen to people? No, Dickinson's speaker says, Death *stopped* for her. Death comes in a carriage, no less. Is it a hearse? Perhaps not. The rather abstruse Death is personified as a somewhat benign sort of chap, one who even exudes "civility." What a comfortable metaphor! There is also another presence in this carriage . . . Immortality. Our speaker is intrigued enough to accompany Death in his mysterious carriage on what becomes a somewhat unfathomable journey.

This iconic poem has inspired me to personify Death as well in the first two sections in this volume. Some of these poems show that Death can be considered as a friend. Sometimes Death comes to visit but does not stay. As I explore in the poems in **Part I: Death Befriended** and in **Part II: Kindred Spirits**, the speaker and Death can mutually decide whether Death goes or stays. Death can be a persuasive friend. Yet we have the power to choose or not choose to go along with Death, even if it is just for the carriage ride. The poems of **Part III: Death Released** further explore Death inside and outside of earthly boundaries. The poems in this section show that fear of death can be transmuted into an experience of enlightened exploration. Once this happens, the soul can have no end of delightful adventures, each and every one of them leading to higher and higher dimensions of love. **Part IV: Soulscape** imagines a panorama of resplendent backdrops for traveling souls.

If, with Death, we follow our own horses' heads, our own path to truth, then time and space will inevitably dissolve into eternity wherein exists the infinite love of a singular Source.

I.

DEATH BEFRIENDED

1. Death Was by Chance Defined for Me One Day

Death was by chance defined for me one day
By Dickinson within her poem sublime
"Because I Could Not Stop For Death," yet time
Until my own death did its truth delay.
Then content of my life came clear to me:
I am one of those children in her ring.
I am of her grain field, gaze lingering
But that day's setting sun I did not see.
Indeed, did earthly sun our carriage pass.
Then with the arms of Death around me tight,
In radiance of a thousand suns I bathed,
My last house in the ground a far morass.
To pure eternal dimension of light,
Her horses brought my soul to home it craved.

2. Rather an Odd Quirk of Death

Rather an odd quirk of Death,
Whom few would call a friend,
That it persists as near as breath
In loyalty without end.

But with this friend we hesitate,
Uncertain of its touch.
We do not stop for Death nor rate
Its presence welcome much.

Yet Death's appeal at times is clear.
It shuns no human ties,
And some to whom it has come near
Gain solace from disguise.

So maybe I'll give Death a break
Whene'er I beckoned be,
And humbly for my new friend's sake
Show best civility.

3.   I Saw Death and Asked Him Why

I saw Death and asked Him why
He kindly stopped for me.
Death said he was just passing by,
Explaining patiently

His carriage would be full next week,
And Immortality
Was glad my company to seek —
Right now a seat was free.

I pondered how to best decide
This opportunity,
Then told Death that this carriage ride
Would not my preference be.

I hastened to add an invite came
From friends and family near
To ride with them — they called my name.
Their love eschewed all fear.

Death bowed politely, tentative,
Sensing my bold resolve,
Then with a wave did gently give
Accord, and fast dissolved.

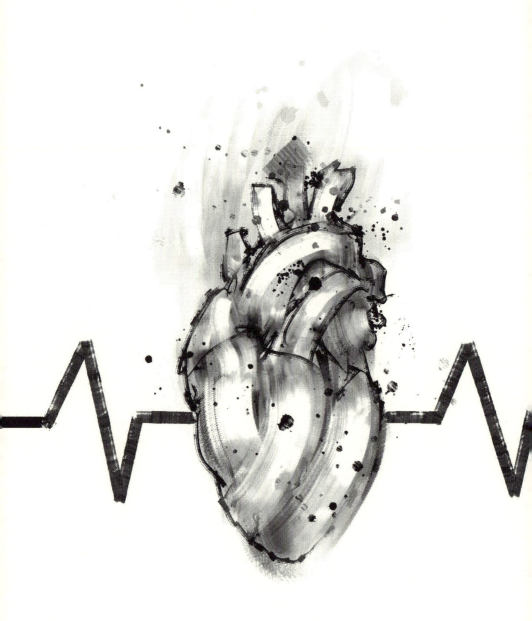

4. When Death Calls I'll Ready Be

When Death calls I'll ready be
With new resolve to treat him well,
And when he rings at my doorbell
I'll invite Death in pleasantly.
Once before Death approached me,
In kindly care my pain helped quell.
So under his elusive spell,
Today's the day all qualms I'll free.
Indeed, when Death came long ago,
Attentive in his special way,
The sights we shared left me aglow.
Yet I refused with Death to play,
But now full favor I'll bestow.
Peaceful in wait for Death I stay.

5. I Meant a Good Hostess to Be

I meant a good hostess to be
When Death stopped by my home kindly.
I did not know this caller well
And was not sure he well knew me.

He was shy, that I could tell,
A tentative press at my doorbell,
But when I thought what Death might claim,
I felt foreboding hard to quell.

Right then more cautious I became.
There stood Death large in my door frame,
A civil caller nonetheless,
Yet somehow I didn't feel the same.

With no incentive to impress,
I told Death I had to confess
Though good hostess I meant to be:
"Please return later and God bless."

6. Death Was Hovering at My Door

Death was hovering at my door
Impatient to come in,
Aware that he would have to wait
In line with closest kin.

He ended up in front of one
Who wept in sharpest pain —
In love for me now totally
Preceded by Death's gain.

In muddled mind, across the room
I sensed the anguish clear
That pierced my kin whom Death defied,
Standing by me too near.

In sudden comfort then I knew
That Death would kindly be,
Coming back one day soon to send
My grieving kin to me.

7. As I Perish Death I See

As I perish, Death I see
Lingering here to walk with me —
Death knows the place in which await
My spirit guides so lovingly.

They vibrate there at portal gate.
I hurry so I won't be late.
They're far away and Death is slow,
To wait for him I hesitate.

I look back, and Death I see
With sudden chill anxiety.
No longer forward can I go —
Death is too weak to set me free.

Heartbroken to my guides I wave,
Trudge back to earth new ways to pave.

8.   Death Do Not Leave Me Behind

Death, do not leave me behind
Too long in this bleak world.
You are the go-between, I find,
Of life stages unfurled.

I want with my beloved to be;
Right now this is not so.
She cannot come back here to me.
May I with her soon go?

Yet if your schedule still precludes
This possibility,
I have resolved to bear earth's feuds
And woes attentively.

Know, Death, when you do come by
For me specifically,
To take me to my beloved,
I Will bless you personally.

9. I Hitchhiked from My Home in Town

I hitchhiked from my home in town,
Wind stirred our poplar tree.
Most drivers passed me with a frown
Until Death stopped for me.

She was hesitant and drove
So slowly I was shocked.
Her great white car did barely move,
While Death and I just talked.

She knew my beloved, my daughter too,
She knew my baby boy —
My love for sweet Death gently grew.
I felt a soothing joy.

Yet coy with me she then became
She turned her car around —
While under a shimmering eastern sun,
Death brought me back to town.

The day was warm, my friends were there —
My heart with peace now surged.
Then Death receded back to where
Her road from mine diverged.

10.   In Autumn on a Raft Death Came

In autumn on a raft Death came —
Thick sturdy logs beneath me lay.
I knew Death could my body claim,
Yet still the choice to go or stay

Remained for me that day to make.
My soul hovered displaced, unsure —
Soft poplars trembled by the lake,
Their whispering rustling soft and pure.

When suddenly a fiery deep
Incarnadine oak tree I saw.
Huge on the western shore it spread
Vast branches, filling me with awe.

To its great roots my soul was drawn —
Death steered her raft to stop nearby.
There sage oak's truth on me did dawn —
With it my soul chose to abide.

11. My Willing Soul is Wooed by Death

My willing soul is wooed by Death,
Fair kingdom that she offers me.
From where I dwell on arid heath,
I'll soon in dateless splendor be.
Over highlands, lakes remote,
We skim on breezes out to sea.
Then, settling on the cosmic boat
Of enigmatic Death, I'm free.
Profound journeys stretch away
Before us in the glittering west.
No longer do I pine to stay
Behind where maelstrom snuffs all rest.
New vibrancies await ahead
As hand in hand with Death I'm led.

12.   Mist-Clad Death Amongst the Myrtles

Mist-clad death amongst the myrtles,
In the distance cries are faint.
A blanket of white blooms encircles
Lovers who with Death acquaint.
As they embrace drenched in ardor,
Myrtle branch by them aligns.
As they woo in darksome grandeur,
Unreserved death them entwines.
Fragrant essence round them curls —
Death's pure face is soft and dark.
Deep sweet secrets it unfurls
As one in Death the lovers hark
To where their love will boundless be,
In realm beyond the myrtle tree.

13. We Do Not Die Without Our Own Consent

We do not die without our own consent:
Nothing occurs but represents our wish.
No matter how we feel of life misspent,
To doubt this truth belies what must nourish.
Can grief be part of joy, or pain of peace?
Can sickness come where holiness abides?
Only when ego's illusions cease,
May we forgo all transitory tides.
No chaos, fear, nor Death did God create;
'Tis only madness that we think it so.
Let us most humbly this thought negate,
In stillness laying self-deception low.
Then He who never left will show again,
When truth to us is known — and only then.

14. Is Death Our Only Guarantee?

Is Death our only guarantee,
More prevalent than love?
I know 'tis not! Rather, I see
Death as a timely glove

That warms my hand as it extends
To love in spirit free —
A fluid warmth — as love transcends —
Death serves exigency.

When frigid cold descends upon
My white hand still as stone,
Death's ashen glove is long since gone,
Yet helped my soul atone.

II.

KINDRED SPIRITS

15. Death Wrapped a Shawl Around My Shoulder

Death wrapped a shawl around my shoulder,
Yet a chill spread through my heart,
Spreading, as the room grew colder —
Bold confidence from me did part.

I called to Death who waited near,
A caregiver for all my needs,
A patient friend sublimely dear
Performing daily kindly deeds.

"Go take a break, you've done enough,"
I cried with new intent resolve.
"I can continue, I am tough,
And in this life I will evolve!"

The warmth of my outburst surprised
Death, and with humble stance he rose,
Removed my shawl, my plea surmised —
Death left me to the life I chose.

16. Death Looked Rather Puzzled

Death looked rather puzzled when I passed him in the hall.
The flock he meant to meet this night bypassed his daily call.
In fact, Death said, it seemed quite clear, there was no one at all
Within this town in need of him, and this did Death appall.

"Be not so proud," I advised Death, "soon with you all will go.
Perhaps though you might reconsider how your gifts do flow.
In fact, it seems that nowadays more human beings know
That you are slave to fate and chance. Death's chains we overthrow!"

Death reflected and mused over my words carefully,
Confessed he never thought himself as intermediary.
Death's eyes were opened, and he saw the king he meant to be
Was superseded by his role as friend to spirits free.

17.   To Death I Was Quite Truculent

To Death I was quite truculent, his goodwill moved me not.
White saucy stars, his companions, did not my interest stir.
When Death's presence nearby I sensed, my manners I forgot.
I blamed him for my troubles and I called him "Saboteur!"
For Death, it seemed, was devious, his aim to ruin joy;
More than once I felt him gloating, plotting who would die.
At times he swooped upon my friends and family to destroy
Their lives with stopless grisly presence, anguished asked I why.
Then one day a revelation came in glistening light;
Vast stars throbbing in the sky caressed my soul with love.
Amongst them Death was mingling, a beacon in the night,
A pearly presence was he, a great lustrous friend above.
Vast centuries have passed since that day when I Death forgave.
Forever grateful am I now, for Death my soul did save.

18.   In the Gloaming Shrewd Death Steals Aloft

In the gloaming shrewd Death steals aloft —
She whispers in the blue light of the day.
I sense her slip by grass-lined marshes soft,
Absorbed through shuttering windows on her way.
Death stalks "l'heure bleue," her transitory friend,
With slant of light at summer solstice brief.
At times the gloaming day seems n'er to end —
Its disingenuous shadows bode no grief.
Then as summer wanes, I feel a chill —
In shortening days blue light is growing dim.
Grim Death slips by me slyly slant until
She usurps light, infests my heart to brim.
Now ghost of illness grows as blue nights fade —
A strengthened specter morphed to Death's handmaid.

19.   Death Told My Doctor to Tell Me

Death told my doctor to tell me
My time on earth was short to be.
Though not afraid of death, oddly,
I did resent her bitterly.

Weak and hopeless, nearing Death,
No one to grieve my dying breath,
All hope that gave my being heft
Had heretofore left me bereft.

Yet now that Death had set my date,
Strangely, no longer did I hate.
My desperate life could now abate;
With Death I would fresh life create.

Now at present, sight is clear
As to the tunnel I draw near,
Awareness dissipating fear —
New realms of love with Death appear.

20. I Saw a Little Grassy Hole

I saw a little grassy hole
Above my head one day
And crept in, having climbed a knoll —
I thought Death might here stray.

Imagined rabbits snuggled by,
My furry forest kin.
As well, the moss was sweet and dry —
I snuggled soft within.

I waited for Death patiently,
Stretched with a cozy sigh.
Soft poplars whispered close to me
A soothing lullaby.

Dear dreams arrived as in the cool
Embrace of green I sank —
Forgot far Death while in that pool
Of nature's love I drank.

21. When I Was Planning for My Funeral

When I was planning for my funeral,
Death a tasteful distance stood —
Sensing my bleak somber mood,
Not yet in its mode eternal.
Respects would be held in a space
Where soothing decor was a balm,
Wallpaper with pastels calm,
Old photos in their windowed case.
Lulled was I by all the genial
Tones and moods and comforts there.
I sighed and let Death's presence fade —
Knowing Death's yoke, there so menial,
Would transmute at crossroads where
My bond with Death would soon be made.

22. My Date with Death Approaches

My date with Death approaches: here I stay
Amidst a clan distraught and wrung with tears.
At night sweet Sleep, Death's kin, takes me away.

Yet no such comfort comes in waking day;
My daylight hours are drenched with wild fears.
My date with Death approaches: here I stay

To ease my grief. My weak pleas hold no sway
As I relive my pain caused through the years.
At night sweet Sleep, Death's kin, takes me away,

And in my dreams Death asks me if she may
Escort me to a realm where no thought sears.
My date with Death approaches: here I stay.

Death's great white car stops by my chamber gray.
Up to my anguished, broken form she nears.
At night sweet Sleep, Death's kin, takes me away.

In dreams this night, no doubts do me gainsay.
I know I soon will hear my angel cheers.
My date with Death approaches: here I stay.
At night sweet Death, Sleep's kin, takes me away.

23.   Death Amongst the Daffodils

Traveling was I along the lane to meet
My loved ones, who had passed already to
That spirit realm infused with gardens sweet,
While I passed earthly blooms with springtime dew.
My spirit guides stood patiently nearby
When suddenly saw I in golden view
A host of daffodils in meadow nigh —
Basking in sun-soaked breezes and I knew
It was my life's departing gift to seize.
The flaxen panorama floated up
In yellowly shimmering shadows past the trees,
Toward the town where my soul was to sup.
Then I and my guides to family table came,
Which bright rolling hills of daffodils did frame.

24. Death I Have Walked in Your Darkening Shadow

Death, I have walked in your darkening shadow;
Your valley gets deeper, more rugged each day.
With dim pathways twisting, yet soothingly hallowed,
No obstacles bar my implacable way.
I fear thee not, Death, for this valley is dappled
With shafts of sweet sunlight on rippling streams.
Though I on these paths with my nightmares have grappled,
On a hill I see yonder a table that gleams.
I climb from your valley, am brought to the table
Full laden with platters of bountiful fare.
Come now sit beside me, Death, if you are able;
Your shadow won't darken the love glowing there.
When with our good host we've supped through the night,
Death, rise with me, please to seek dawn's ruby light!

25. Death and Angels Corresponded

Death and angels corresponded
When my case before them came.
Over me their forces bonded,
Waiting soft to call my name.
My first inkling of transition
Dipped into my being that day,
Though still my body's inhibition
Begged me not from earth to stray.
Now my angels gathered near me
Joyous, resonant, filled with love.
Courteous Death stood by discreetly,
Keeper of my treasure trove.
Then Death and angels descended —
In bliss with them my soul ascended.

26. When in Death I Leave My Shell

When in Death I leave my shell
And go to distant realms,
I travel in angelic knells
Where beauty overwhelms.

There cordial company awaits
In high vibration rapt —
Welcomes me in astral state,
No longer earthbound trapped.

I savor souls in mutual bliss.
I frisk in playful joy.
Then my spirit blows a kiss
To face eternal day.

27.   How Good to Be Safe in Graveyards

How good to be safe in graveyards,
In dark closed urns to stay,
No longer to bear the yoke
Of burdens that dismay.

One could then await their angels,
An afternoon to play.
How wonderful with them to be
Included straightaway.

Oh joy, to be with my soul guardians,
Rollick without fray,
And when dusk calls my angels home,
To go with them I may.

28. Death Is Like Changing Avatars

Death is like changing avatars
In all those games we play —
No big deal just as long
As we can win the fray —
Just as long as we remember
Reasons why we lose,
And learn from the mistakes we make,
Then Death can be our muse.

III.

DEATH RELEASED

29. Oppenheimer, Einstein Discuss

Oppenheimer, Einstein discuss
The earthly bomb that could our world destroy.
Deep concern is held by each man who
In searching his soul, speaking his fears, must
Staunch by any means he can employ,
Visions of rippling flames our planet through.
There is an episode of Dr. Who
Written by children in oddly prescient voice,
Where Einstein is in rabid jest contrived,
Transformed into a hapless squid-faced Ood
From a slave race, chanting repeatedly
"Death is the only answer." "Death is the
Only answer." Then he makes the choice
To time-travel back to nineteen forty-five.

30. Reflections on Jesus Christ Superstar

Followers who so reverent were
In Superstar become a blur,
Transmogrified to screeching curs
And Jesus is alone.

In speaking truth he's damned by all
Of Pilate's peers as weak and small —
Tortured, bloodied, made to crawl
And Jesus is alone.

His message damned him while he lived
And yet he judged not, did forgive,
In brilliance saw his oneness bridged
To us, compassion sown.

A tearful child his mother holds,
Cries he would have let Jesus go —
But in time his purpose grows
To be as Jesus known.

Where did the soul of Jesus go?
Is it in next dimension now,
A guide in universal flow
Where no one is alone?

31. Consider Phlebas

Consider Phlebas, ill-starred, leaving shore,
A trader sailing in life's game,
Unafraid of the sea's glittering roots, for
Profit and loss blithely came.

Plain fishermen who in Galilee strove,
Abundance from wanton sea caught,
In miracle bounty replete to behoove
Apostles who livelihood sought.

Ingenuous beings on seas of the cosmos
Head windward when into the waves,
Entering the whirlpool, fearing no ghosts
Nor cosmic nor watery graves.

32. Those Are Pearls That Were His Eyes

Those are pearls that were his eyes,
Live gems that cannot see —
As old Tiresias shimmering wise
Are creatures drowned at sea.

Horrific death is drowning at sea.
Yet beautiful spirits there be
That arise from the drowned past that moment of dread
Departing precipitously.

Those are pearls that were his eyes,
Eyes that now timeless can see —
Prescient jewels of worth and rebirth,
A treasure for humanity.

33. Death Led Me to My Pool Angels

I saw glistening pools in the gray barrens lie
Like great golden angels, surrounded by dew.
My kindred new moon in the far western sky
Was paling and fading from tenuous view.

Death waited kindly, and I grew ecstatic
As this final vision above I beheld.
My vibrant perception expanded like magic,
As Death led me to where my pool angels dwelled.

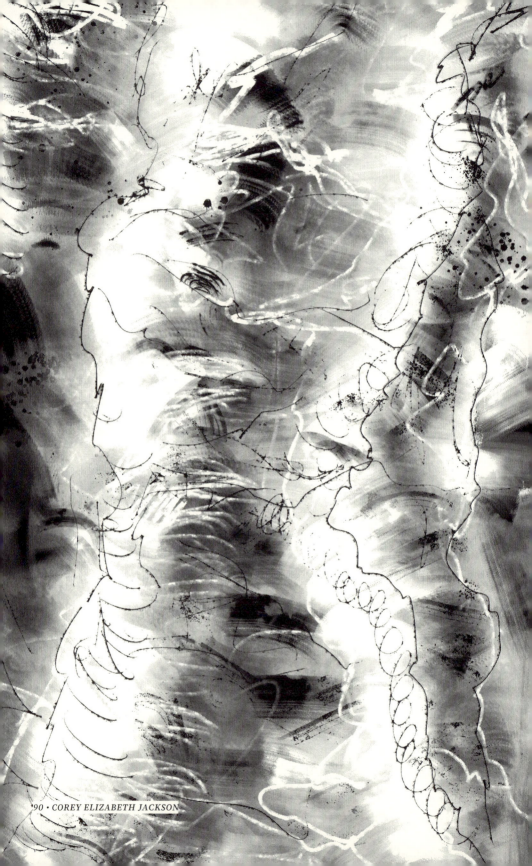

'90 • *COREY ELIZABETH JACKSON*

34.   In a Mystic Dreamlike Lake

In a mystic dreamlike lake
I froth midst sentient waves,
Rusty and cerulean hues
Surrounding me with ease.

Their surging swirling active grace
Inspires my awed intent
To grasp this watery carnival
By dream dimensions sent.

In murky distance through the foam
And churning ripples sweet,
My rapt awareness knows no fear
Of surging watery feat.

Bright glint of rust on waves subsides;
Bronzed sun dips down afar.
My soul now goes from foam to flight,
To swim with kindred stars.

35. Above Lake Ontario the Butterflies Appear

Above Lake Ontario the butterflies appear
In late summer — languid breeze is soft and warm and sweet.
Black and amber wings are fluttering by the water near
To sandy shore at Ward's Island in twos and threes they meet.

Pleasure boats are anchored in a line within the cove,
Sun-drenched owners reaching down to bobbing dinghies tied.
Between them and the jutting land mercurial monarchs rove —
Funneling exuberantly in burnished streaks they glide.

I swim, knowing spirit clans by these totems are held,
Take comfort my ancestors passed are reaching out to me.
Their souls in transit brush my being and then with others meld,
Souls in monarch butterflies connecting tangibly.

Suddenly on my wave-dipped hand — a single butterfly
Alights. In submerged joy I bless my soulmate passing by.

36. On Mother Earth

On Mother Earth our spirit grows
As Covid deaths moved to impose
Bleak tyranny, with scant escape
Since our masked world formed its shape
In blight we never could suppose.

Stalwart resolve within us shows;
In hearts our human family sows
Deep seeds of love, a new soulscape
On Mother Earth.

Hearts bloom with care from seeds we chose;
Behind all masks our essence glows.
Around us all a celestial cape,
Protecting every being, doth drape.
As One we now our fears oppose
On Mother Earth.

37.   With Covid Deaths We Can More Widely See

With vision like the eagle soaring high,
With Covid deaths we can more widely see.
The human race is One, we can't deny.

To heal our shattered world we ever try,
And grow we shall, for we are always free,
With vision like the eagle soaring high.

The sinkhole of indifference we decry;
We serve each other, send light outwardly.
The human race is One, we can't deny.

'Midst Covid deaths there stands a portal by,
Now open to wiser humanity,
With vision like the eagle soaring high.

In harsh pandemic maelstrom we rely
On daily rituals, deepening spiritually.
The human race is One, we can't deny.

No cenotaph required, for now we fly!
Grim Covid chaos transmutes energy
With vision like the eagle soaring high.
The human race is One, we can't deny.

38. Barbie Could Not Stop for Death

Barbie could not stop for Death, she went
Into the Real World to save her own.
Full of hope she boldly made her way.
Each earthly adventure made apparent
Her imperfections. Seeds of doubt were sown.
In Real World she did not want to stay.
Yet she saw Barbie Land was just a play,
A delusion where she had no control,
A land where bland perfection morphed to strife
And left her ordered being in disarray.
Irrepressible Thoughts of Death Barbie
She became, in despair harboring
The will to change. She retrieved her soul —
Only then embraced she choice and life.

39. Ode to Marilyn

The dark oozed odious Outfit goons, who
Heinously chloroformed you.
Snuffed with poisoned cruelty
Was your beauty, transformed to

Ghoulish snapshots, covert, grim,
Congealing radiant glow.
Still these long years past, your pure
And shimmering essence flows.

Your heart was snared in web of graft,
Your soul in splendor wreathed.
Ah, dear angel, blessed forever,
Rest in loving peace.

40. Dying on Spadina

He sprawls by a pub on historic Spadina,
Head sunken deep in his arm.
Our tour group in Kensington passes around him,
Glances away in alarm.

He swears bitter tirade into gray debris.
We marvel at dancers that jive
On the new El Mocombo sign, raspberry neon —
Recall that the Stones played there live.

Grinding cries wretched in dying despair
Continue behind us forlorn.
Door of the Krispy Kreme opposite opens
Across busy street on the corner.

Young man emerges, drawn to keening brother,
Puts cup and small bag by his hand,
Brushes the stiff arm, recrosses Spadina,
As tour group moves on to sites grand.

41. Owl Ensconced on Oaken Branch

Owl ensconced on oaken branch,
A wingèd spirit rare.
His gaze is wisdom: calm, intent,
Bewitching and aware.

Soulful and implacable,
His feathered stillness bright
Is outlined by cerulean sky,
A beacon of the night.

Behind stark owl a full moon glows,
Casts vectored rays of light,
And yon in inky distance pierce
Sweet stars his friends in flight;

But tawny owl remains transfixed
Upon his earthly tree,
Before he soars in deathly realm,
Sage spirit flying free.

Written after reading in Lucy Maud Montgomery's journals of the death of her second son, Hugh, in August 1914, one week after the start of World War I.

42.   When First I Saw My Baby Boy

When first I saw my baby boy, great joy in me arose.
So plump and dear and dimpled was his round and downy head;
So perfect were his little fingers and his minute toes.
I reached out thrilled to nestle him lovingly in my bed.

In horror saw I suddenly my babe's unmoving form.
White and waxen limbs so still, his soul had bid farewell.
My being in agony despaired, my son no longer warm.
Almost killed was I in torment, trapped in deepest hell.

Now every day I go to see his tiny forlorn plot,
Know his wee face 'neath a ground that smothers all his cries.
At twilight must I leave him there with loving mother not,
His only lonely company the space of autumn skies.

My broken heart yet steadies me despite my son it grieves,
For part of it stays on his grave with autumn's whispering leaves.

43. As I Abate My Fear of Death

As I abate my fear of death
Through darkening streets I roam,
The cobblestones beneath my feet
Uneven in the gloam.

Stabbed by cold and damp I turn
My collar 'gainst the grip
Of cruel fear countering resolve —
My faltering footsteps slip —

Suddenly jagged neon lights
Flash on my cobbled way,
Brightly jabbing faceless crowds
That moan and bend and sway.

But soft — a dim light haloes from
The street lamp where I lean
Beside a gate — as night descends —
My heart soars, now serene.

Instantly the gate outspreads
As if through tunnelling time,
Absorbing all us beings as One
In dimensions sublime.

44. "Not Dead" Says the Plaque on the Park Bench

"Not Dead" says the plaque on the park bench on my walk
At the summit of the path on Sheppard's Hill.
I stop in my tracks, riveted, and turned to look more closely,
The forest round me glinting deep and still.

The message on the plaque continues: "Temporary resting place"
A woman with her "furry family"
Appears to have passed over to the other side while walking
Her three dogs "Maggie, Bentley and Mini."

I pause and sit down, contemplating. Surely these dear pets
Can sense her essence intuitively
Alive, and cherish this spot by the forest deep and still
When now with her close kin they walking be.

"Not Dead" says the plaque on the park bench on my walk,
A truth known by her loving dogs. Now she
Must be comforting her loved ones as they read the plaque, then sense
Her presence, which surrounds them spiritually.

45. Housefly Buzzes at my Window

Housefly buzzes at my window,
Falters on a frantic path,
Along tethering two dimensional
Surface of unyielding glass.

At my desk, I see beneath
Fly's prison pane, his escape clear —
Open space where freedom beckons
To aeolian sun splashed air.

In wild, dizzy desperation,
Fly now bounces, springs away
Into miracle third dimension —
On flat death trap does not stay.

Then — in timeless sovereignty —
Fly imperceptibly shifts
Below window's deadly barrier —
Outside to sweet fearless bliss.

In slow somnolent circles he
Now undulates hypnotically —
Then, buzzing ever, dips to me
And flees, skirting eternity —

46.   The Old Native Chieftain from Forests Among

The old native chieftain from forests among
Deep sapphire lakes of the tribe,
With death approaching instinctively covets
The spot where his transition lies.

Reclining in solitude 'midst verdant hills
Where spirits more closely abide,
He's drawn to rare lightness where portals are linked
To diverse dimensions of sky.

His people do grieve his departure foretold,
But accept obligation to stay
Far below near the shore, at the teepee fire circled
Giving prayers on their leader's last day.

His angels do beckon from heavenly heights,
Drawing near as his soul rises blessed,
Leaving his stark and still body in grace
With face gently turned to the west.

47.   To My Sister Valerie

In my dream I lay transfixed
By vision pierced in light:
A pure white horse before me went,
His mane in shadow caught.

As he moved further away,
I made no effort to
Catch up with him. He awed me so,
Then vanished from my view.

I stood amidst billowing clouds
Alert in reverie,
Then was conscious of a creature
Curling close by me.

Unafraid, I saw a lightness
Part the clouds, and lo —
I saw and felt the pliant fleece
Of a gentle ivory lamb.

He curved around my right leg in
Affection sweet and sage.
He raised his head and looked at me —
The beauty of that face!

With eyes iridescent he
Gave solace to me, then
I wept — embraced by emerald love
From realm beyond my ken.

Written after reading Dickinson's "Safe in their Alabaster Chambers".

48. We Are Not Dots on a Disc of Snow

We are not dots on a disk of snow.
No alabaster tombs
Enclose our cold and vacant brow
Nor substitute as home.

Along with those from humble grave
We rove castles with glee.
We tread as One in spirit brave
With birds and babbling bee.

We are not dots on a disc of snow,
But rich as bright diadems dear,
Timelessly present as firmaments row —
No sagacity perished here!

IV.

SOULSCAPE

Written in memory of our beloved theatre family who perished in a traffic accident on November 22, 2022 near Peterborough, Ontario.

49. Full of Vibrant Joy the MacHarts Came

Full of vibrant joy the MacHarts came
To Queensville Players Theatre for our show,
High School Musical, sparked by their flame
Of energy and love and dazzling glow.
Riddick as Troy our star shone on us all
With hard work, talent and connection warm.
Jon as Coach did everyone enthrall
With spoofing antics and comedic form.
Stefphanie stepped in as well to be
Both in our play and bracing us with care,
And to our show came Rowghan cheerfully,
Enriching every scene that she did share.
Oh dear MacHarts, you soothe our hearts now sore.
Abide in peace, we love you evermore.

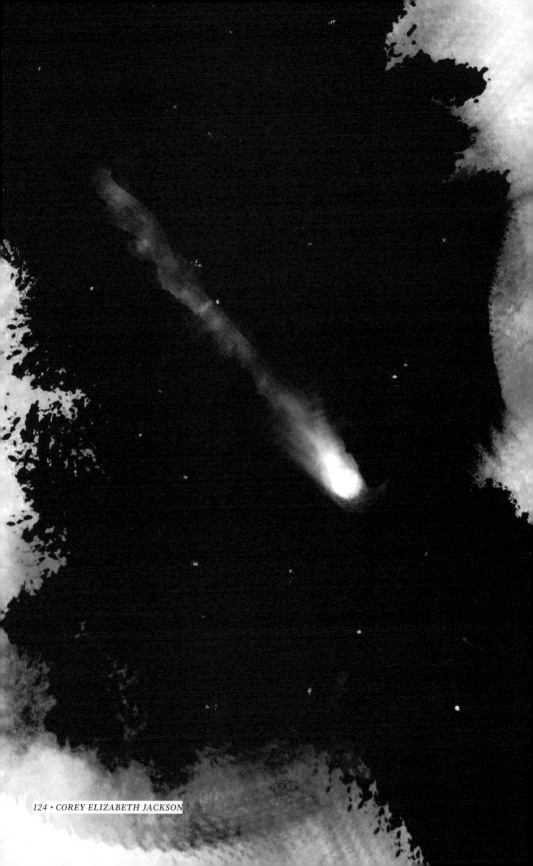

50. Let My Soul Go When Required

Let my soul go when required.
Send it to the stars
To further travel reinspired
Beyond all locks and bars,
To reincarnate richer still
Through every unlocked door,
On all paths to atonement till
Soul knows Source evermore.

KAY ELIZABETH JACKSON

51. My Soul Leaves Body Floats from Home

My soul leaves body, floats from home
Into cedars above,
Hovers momentarily
Absorbed in sentient grove.

Surrounded by sweet glowing night,
It tingles in suspense,
Slips past sleeping kin, takes flight,
Departs from ego tense.

Great undulating lake it skirts
Then soars into the skies,
Corporeal form left far behind
In roistering woodland sighs.

Intrepid astral soul leaps clear
Beyond wood, lake and land,
Stops poised aloft our planet dear
To spread in cosmos grand,

To bask in stillness soft among
Our primal common clan,
Who thrills my soul has gladly come
To universal span.

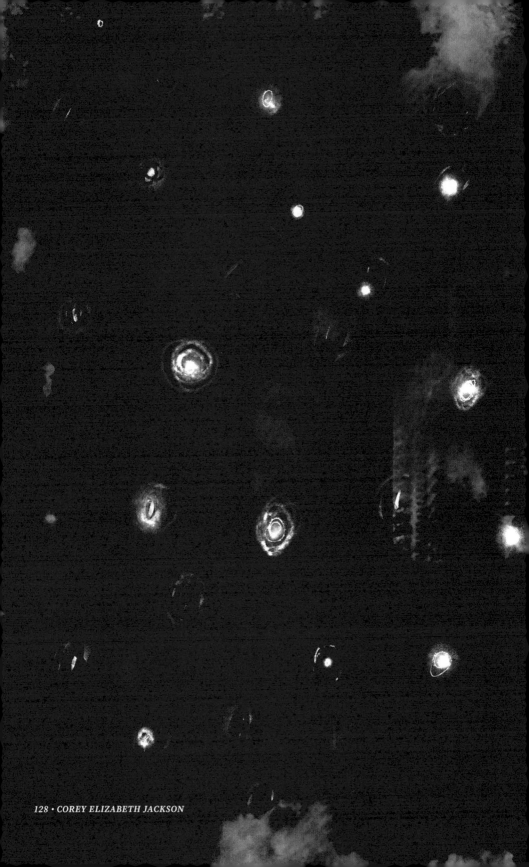

52.   My Essence Seeks That Static State

My essence seeks that static state
Where stillness waxes prime,
Amidst meadow brook and dell
Eluding space and time.
Whispering senses link to realms
Oft hovering in plain sight,
But simply shadowed by my mind
Before it harbors flight.

53.   Reflections in McKenzie Marsh

Spread my soul through willow branches drooping languidly
By the marsh's winding stream where bustling beavers be.
Lift my soul up to black walnuts ripe with kernels plump;
Let my soul hike bending pathways in the marsh I see.

Let my soul bow to crown clover — regal — rosy — fair.
Show my soul sweet turtleheads that spice the potent air.
Sink my soul into the glade where pale birches wave;
Let my soul rest in the grove which gentle deer do share.

My soul bypasses clanging trains that in the distance roar,
Ascends beyond far city's hum to where rapt eagles soar.
Soft my soul slips back to me rejoicing joyfully,
At home in McKenzie Marsh where it lives evermore.

54. Soak My Soul in Babbling Brooks

Soak my soul in babbling brooks
'Mongst springtime woods and dales
To join deep oceans blue and grand
And hobnob with the whales.

Spread my soul on tops of lilacs
In meadows newly green.
Slide my soul amongst the trillium
Of spring flowers queen.

Hike my royal soul up mountains,
Rugged — watchful — kind —
Home as blooming souls and flowers
Through their passes wind.

Send my soul into the skies
To permeate as one
With other spring souls venturing,
And from which all souls come.

55.   Sink My Soul Through Frozen Ponds

Sink my soul through frozen ponds,
Pristine new fallen snow,
As through a cloud solidified
And pressed into each row
Of jagged ripples now caressed
Into a blanket smooth.
My soul abides in whitened chill
Under dusk's hovering glow.

My soul spreads soft to every stone
Around pond's downy wrap,
Travels deeply, swiftly through
All earthly shores and traps —
To soar eternally with ease
To realms as yet untold,
Still quivering with the ecstasy
A portal pond bestowed.

56. Let My Soul Slip into Oceans

Let my soul slip into oceans
Pierced by sunlight from on high,
Comforted by creatures gliding
Glad at home where mollusks lie.
My soul travels with sea clans,
Sleek dapper dolphins, octopi.
My soul skips in riotous splendor
Through dimensions of the sea.

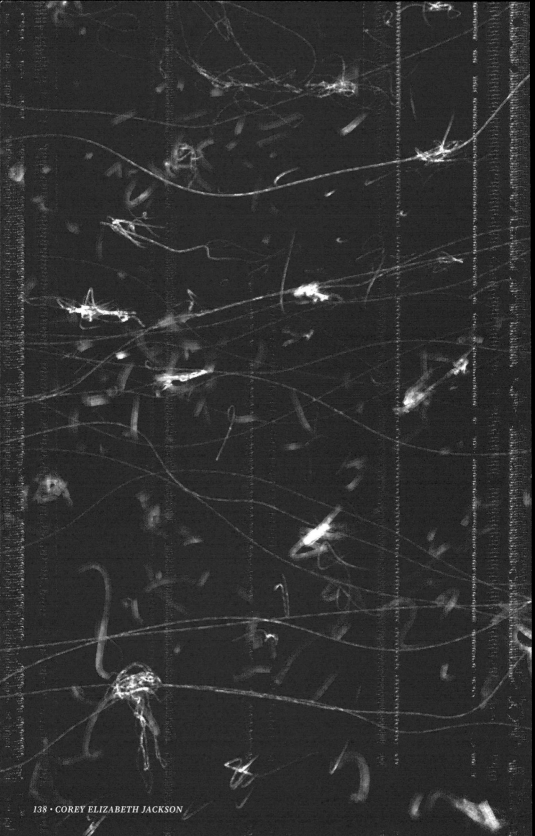

57.   Dipping Into Oceans Blue

Dipping into oceans blue
And dipping out by day:
At night each dip becomes a dive
To where deep stillness lays.
There nautical life permeates;
Wise fluid spirits glow
Wherein the dead of watery sphere
To transcendence they flow.

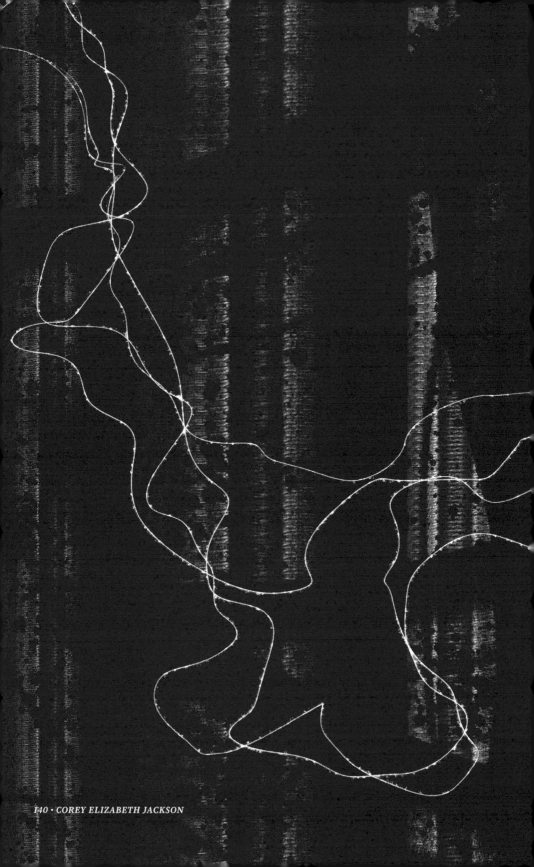

58. My Soul Is at Home in the Depths of the Ocean

My soul is at home in the depths of the ocean;
My soul is at home in the cosmos above,
Always adventuring, seeking to grow and
Wreathing my body in infinite love.

My soul permeates every stone on our Earth,
Every plant, every pod, every intricate cave.
My soul permeates every star of our universe,
Each atom of galaxies beautifully made.

My soul befriends others, my constant companions
In bubbling joy of creational flair,
At home in dimensions of endless proportions
Traveling timelessly, yet ever here.

59. I Go to the Place Where Stillness Waits

I go to the place where stillness waits anticipating me;
She is my friend who's always there no matter where I be.
She rests in azure light in my soul ever patiently,
Because she knows that she and I will visit regularly.

She often waits for me upon the boat to Bali Hai
Or on a soft dark moonlit lake where rippling wishes lie.
She travels with me on my raft where streaming waters sigh,
Floating to notes of native flutes sweet quivering from on high.

Timeless stillness glows upon the distant mountains fair;
She dances lightly round the stars in delicate steps I share.
In kindred night, our good day done, she flows back with me where
In my cave I with stillness sleep caressed by forest air.

60. My Soul Is Off to Visit Chums

My soul is off to visit chums
Residing past horizons fair,
Spanning centuries, dipping into
Solitary hermit stars,
Passing entities in transit,
Reaching out to worlds dear,
Perching rapt in hubs of space —
Dancing on the face of Mars.

61.   A Hut in Deepest India

A hut in deepest India,
Doorway to inky skies,
In balmy air is alert, crackling,
Rich with resonant sighs.

In nearby village eerie, sleeping
Restless curs turn mute.
About me tingling space vibrates,
As by a quivering lute.

Far Sirius shimmers, beckoning
In kindly welcome clear,
Inviting me to meet pure souls
In sixth dimension there.

Now on my mat I go in death,
By astral journey blest,
To meet compatriots beyond
My hut, my earthly nest.

62.   Soft Dear Balm of Ebony Night

Soft dear balm of ebony night
Caresses me as I take flight,
My soul in death now in clear sight
Of radiant stars nearby.

No more does ego my soul taint.
No more do chains of cruel restraint
Hold me locked as I acquaint
With source, bid Earth good-bye.

Sentient galaxies urge me forth:
Star creators, giving birth
To hubs of conscious sublime worth,
A welcome to their sky.

My consciousness in rapture glows
Embraced by universal flows.
My being soaked in love light grows.
No longer ask I why.

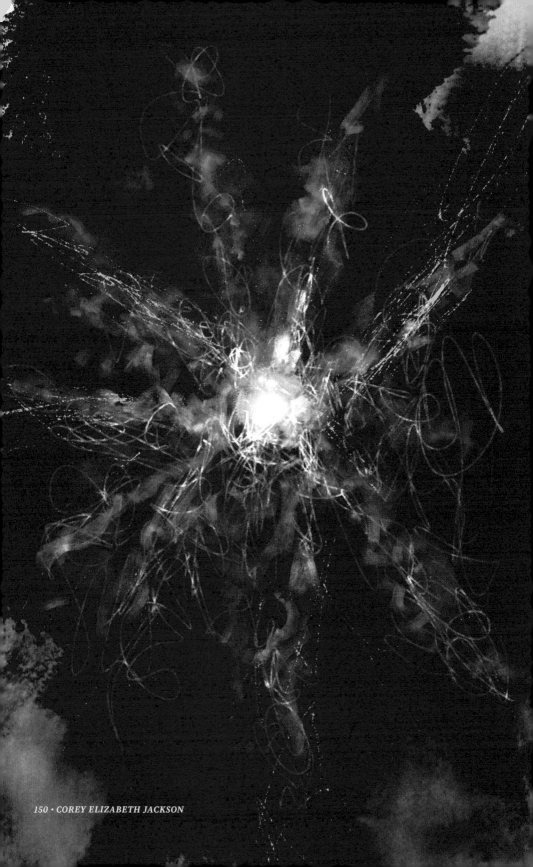

63.   Death in One Quick Quantum Leap

Space of stillness ever round me —
Tableau for my soul —
Is filled with soft vibrations humming,
Strengthened by the shoal

Of all unique souls seeding planets —
Galaxies beyond —
Of all souls in our loving cosmos
Spread to universe edge.

Then in one quick quantum leap
My soul expands to reach
Into familiar stillness past —
Where multiverses stretch.

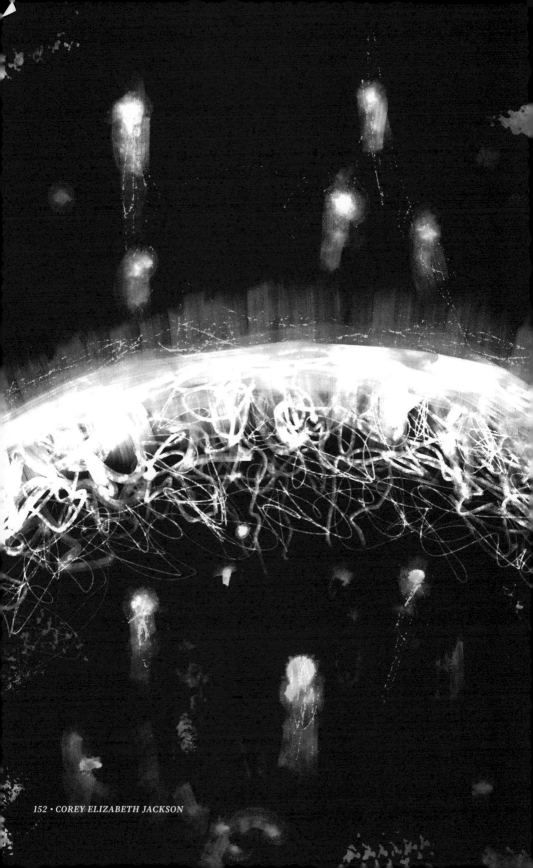

64. Far in Elliptical Galaxy Realms

Souls in higher dimensions proliferate
Far in elliptical galaxy realms,
Aligned in our universe blissfully, peacefully
Ready as vanguard, alert at the helm,
Darting to new universes with burgeoning,
Resonantly vibrating, harmonized souls —
Ever expanding and ever enriching,
Joyously entangled love-sharing goals.

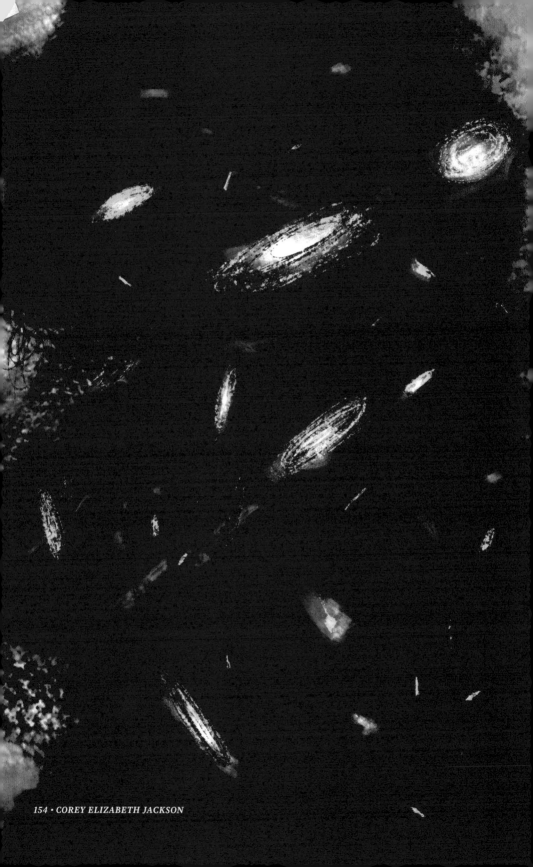

65. Galaxies with Memories

Galaxies with memories
Befriending each their kind,
Sentient, compassionate,
Through universes wind —
Caring for their children stars
Fathers of planets and moons,
Wisdom of mothers in galaxies all
Spiral, elliptical, merged.

66. Awaiting the Solar Flare

Infinite intelligence let us align
With other beings when volcanoes flow.
Permit us in mutual love to entwine
To strengthen each other for sun's earthly blow.
With fire and brimstone now prophesied near,
Support us by taking good people away.
Release all our souls to sweet spirit guides dear
To await a new Earth in our heavenly bay.
Then plant us afresh on our planet so fair,
Kissed newly with tourmaline light on all land,
Her oceans now brimming with life everywhere,
As humans together in joy and peace stand.
Even more we implore from the depths of each heart
To know we are One and from nothing apart!

67.   Eyes That See Beyond This World

Eyes that see beyond this world,
Lips that speak of love,
Growing numbers sensing that
Our time has come to rove.

Travelers we will be soon
To join our distant kin,
Who wait for us with open arms
To welcome us within,

To homes of high vibrations pure
In lands of hope and care,
On planets in live galaxies
Where all beings love light share.

68.   When Multiple Trillions of Years Have Passed

When multiple trillions of years have passed from now,
When our universe holds no life-giving sea,
Black holes abound where stars no longer glow —
All sparks of galaxies have ceased to be.

Yet infinite intelligence still reigns,
No vibration of perfect love destroyed.
Eternity its life force never feigns,
No atom in its might is rendered void.

Now each soul in its own singular life
Retains its essence to infinity.
Spreads fractally forever without strife,
No room for death, no love light entropy.

Thus, never is Creator left alone —
Absorbed within all souls forever known.

Epilogue

I am in the moment —
I savor the present
And bask in the wonder of now —

A Second — condensed — contains
All life's Abundance —
Death will come soon enough so

Endowed ever faithfully
With full Sovereignty —
Always within me consigned —

I revel in myriad
Moments that happen in
Barely a speck of our Time —

Acknowledgments

Thank you, Platypus Publishing and Matt Rud, for giving me the boost in confidence I needed to publish this book. Matt made me comfortable with the idea of using the Reedsy marketplace where I found the experts I needed to help me fulfill my vision for this book's design and content. Thank you, Reedsy.

Thank you to my husband Jim, who has been my rock. He has always supported my writing one hundred percent, and has helped make every day run more smoothly during even my most intense hours spent to make this book happen. Thank you to our sons, Brian and Brent, who have also been continually interested in my poems and whose tech support has helped keep me sane.

To my mother, who gave me my love of literature . . . I remember when I was seven years old, my older sisters and I marveling over a small chapbook in which a short poem penned by our mother had been published. We simply couldn't believe that our mother's name and her poem could be printed in a real honest-to-goodness book!

So many heartfelt memories surfaced when Brooke Conroy passed on to me the picture of her boyfriend, Riddick MacHart, to whom, with his family, this book is dedicated. Thank you, Brooke, for your staunch support, and may your path be ever blessed.

The heart and soul of The Ontario Poetry Society's Bunny Iskov has for many years provided me with constant encouragement and advice. Bunny's love of poetry always shines out clearly, and for me she has been an integral source of inspiration.

Thank you so much to my warm-hearted and talented correspondent James A. Tweedie at The Society of Classical Poets. Jim has given me much appreciated advice on publishing my book, and his gracious and informative letters and commentary have been integral in boosting my confidence in my poetry.

The editing advice and ongoing enthusiastic support of Ivy Schweitzer, an editor and director of The Emily Dickinson International Society Bulletin, is truly appreciated. It was an honor to be asked by Ivy to contribute an article for the Bulletin's *Poet to Poet* series in their Fall 2024 publication.

To my phenomenally talented illustrator, Daniel Schmelling, whose inimitable, cosmic and surreal pictorial creations impacted me instantly when I first saw them. I knew that Daniel was the only illustrator for me, and his pictures give me new inspiration every time I see them.

It was a challenge to know how to connect with readers who would be interested in reading my book. My profuse thanks go to my advisor Liz Dubelman for her calm and steady assistance, and for her helpful, patient explanations of all the information she has suggested to facilitate sharing my book with others.

Much appreciation and thanks go to my editor Michael Martin, whose sound and unobtrusive suggestions helped to clear away rough edges in my work. Michael's positive words about my poetry were always greatly appreciated, fueling my resolve to continue my writing.

Thank you, Ashley Santoro, for being so terrific to work with and for all your awesome ideas for the interior design of this book. It was so exciting to see every poem and picture come alive like magic on the page due to your exceptional talents.

Lastly, my sincere and devoted thanks go to my friends and family who have so generously supported my poems and have been profuse and creative in their comments and reviews. I am grateful from the bottom of my heart, and I cherish you all.

FOLLOW ME

https://soulscapepoetry.substack.com/

Made in United States
Troutdale, OR
11/21/2024

24685203R10101